MW00749364

TAYLOR INSTITUTION LIBRARY

Treasures of the Taylorian

Series Two: Writers in Residence

Volume 2

Yoko Tawada
in Dialogue

Edited by Christoph Held, Henrike
Lähnemann, and Alexandra Lloyd

Series editor: Henrike Lähnemann

Taylor Institution Library, Oxford, 2018

Published in June 2018 by Taylor Institution Library.

Copyright © Taylor Institution Library 2018

http://www.bodleian.ox.ac.uk/taylor

A number of digital downloads to accompany the edition are available from *https://www.bodleian.ox.ac.uk/taylor/about/exhibitions-and-publications*. They include:

- Video introductions to the exhibition
- Podcasts of the texts
- Open Access Ebook

The cover image is from the German and Japanese texts by Yoko Tawada published in this books. Special thanks are due to konkursbuch Verlag Claudia Gehrke for generously granting the right to use the original text of *Akzent*. The Japanese texts are published by kind permission of Yoko Tawada.

Typesetting, digital edition and cover design by Emma Huber, Subject Consultant for German, Taylor Institution Library

ISBN be 978-0-9954564-3-3

Taylor Institution Library, St Giles, Oxford, OX1 3NA

Table of Contents

YOKO TAWADA

DAAD WRITER IN RESIDENCE AT THE UNIVERSITY OF OXFORD
17 FEBRUARY TO 2 MARCH 2017

Exhibition Launch, 17 Feb, 5pm, Voltaire Room, Taylorian. The exhibition is open to Bodleian Card holders until 2 March.

German Reading, 22 Feb, 5.30pm, Room 2, Taylorian.

Multilingual Reading (German and Japanese with English Translations) and **Panel Discussion** on 'Poetics of Translation', 28 Feb, 5.30pm, Doctorow Room, St Edmund Hall.

Ill. 1: Poster designed by Lydia Pryce-Jones, issue desk supervisor at the Taylorian, showcasing the range of sponsors from the German Academic Exchange Service (DAAD) to the AHRC Open World Research Initiative 'Creative Multilingualism'

Preface: Exhibitions at the Taylorian
Emma Huber

The Faculty of Modern Languages at Oxford University has an established tradition of using original library materials (including early printed books) not only for research but also for teaching at all levels. The Taylor Institution Library works closely with academics and students, ensuring that acquisitions support their research interests and projects, such as the writer-in-residence scheme.

The Library supports scholars at all career stages to realise exhibition projects. The first booklet in this series was linked with an exhibition which presented a new take on Shakespeare's sonnets by Ulrike Draesner, another Oxford Writer in Residence. Librarians provide assistance and guidance in the practicalities of preparing an exhibition, and help to promote it both online and by designing posters. They prepare captions and display text and install the exhibition, as well as advising on book handling and care, and assisting in the selection of material.

The library has supported a number of exhibitions arising from History of the Book projects by masters' students, of which the Yoko Tawada exhibition is an example. The curation of this exhibition was done by student Sheela Mahadevan.

Exhibitions in the Taylor Insitution Library are held in the Voltaire Room, a specialist reading room, and we are grateful for the patience of readers while exhibitions are set up, and while visitors look at the items on display. We would also like to record our thanks to all the sponsors of the Writer in Residence scheme, without whom the exhibition would not have been possible. We hope many more will follow.

Yoko Tawada in Oxford
Christoph Held

The works of the Japanese writer Yoko Tawada, who lives in Germany and writes in both German and Japanese, demand the suspension of common concepts of reading, understanding, and thinking. Her translingual writing is based on a playful and, at the same time, critical handling of language and various processes of translation: from one language into another, from thoughts into text or sounds, from sounds into text and vice versa. In many of her texts, the linguistic material is taken apart, alienated, and recomposed, in order to achieve new modes of expression, and raise its poetic potential. Through such a deconstructive and productive transformation, her language consistently eludes conventional principles of meaning and its attribution, and thereby opens up a space for criticism and creativity where national and mono-cultural patterns of language, thinking, and identity can be challenged.

Given the current trans-nationalisation of all spheres of life on the one hand, and an alarming worldwide return to concepts of nationhood and cultural borders on the other, the discussion and stimulation of this creative multilingualism can play a key role in social and educational contexts. The fact that the development of its potential for new creative ways of building identities and pluralising values is primarily taking place on an aesthetic-linguistic, i.e. literary, level is also significant in times when academic fields such as Modern Languages and Literary Studies have come under pressure to justify their work. The engagement with transcultural and translingual literature, such as that of Tawada, in the context of higher education enables students to discover, develop and use the social, political, and didactic potential of their own multilingualism as a powerful source of creativity, criticism, and emancipated conceptions of identity.

In 2017, we invited Tawada to the University of Oxford and organised a series of events, in which students were given an invaluable opportunity to discuss with her issues of translation between cultures and differing language systems as well as questions of multilingualism and identity that are central to many of her texts. When we prepared the programme, it was our ambition to give it a transdisciplinary focus that would do justice to the transcultural and multilingual nature of her works. This ambition is reflected in the contents of this book which is the result of some of the events during Tawada's visit, and combines contributions from students of Modern Languages, Oriental Studies, and English.

The project was made possible by the superb German Academic Exchange Service (DAAD) Writer-in-Residence Programme which gives universities in the UK and Ireland the opportunity to invite writers from Germany and involve them in seminars, workshops, and readings. Alongside the DAAD, we would particularly like to thank the Faculty of Medieval and Modern Languages, the Taylor Institution Library, and St Edmund Hall for their generous support.

Ill. 2: Yoko Tawada at the Natural History Museum

Catalogue: Introduction

Henrike Lähnemann

One of the exciting things about teaching and researching in Oxford is the opportunity to work with the unique collections across the libraries and museums. The Masters students in Medieval and Modern Languages have the opportunity to take a course called 'Palaeography, History of the Book, and Digital Humanities' which gives them the chance to develop their own project based on Oxford holdings.

Sheela Mahadevan, one of the Master of Studies students in Modern Languages 2016–17, who herself comes from a multilingual background, decided to base her project on publications by Yoko Tawada looking at them as book objects which creatively meet the challenge of presenting books in multiple languages — and even different scripts. She curated an exhibition combining it with the holdings from the Taylorian collections from different periods and genres, showcasing different ways of presenting linguistic diversity on the page. She also wrote the exhibition catalogue on which her essay is based.

Ill. 3: Display Case at the Taylorian Institution Library

Ill. 4: *Sheela Mahadevan and Christoph Held setting up the exhibition*

Von der Muttersprache zur Sprachmutter: Yoko Tawada's Creative Multilingualism

Sheela Mahadevan

Yoko Tawada was born in 1960 in Tokyo, Japan. From 1982, she did an MA in German literature at Hamburg University, followed by a PhD at Zurich University. Germany is now her home: after living in Hamburg for 22 years, Tawada moved to Berlin in 2006, where she still lives. She writes in both German and Japanese, with the nature of her bilingualism a prominent feature in her work.

Tawada works intensively with German dictionaries when she writes. These are two of those she uses most:

Dornseiff, Franz, and Alfred. Gerstenkorn. Der deutsche Wortschatz nach Sachgruppen. 3. Neubearb. Aufl. ed. Berlin: W. De Gruyter &, 1943.

Kluge, Friedrich, and Elmar. Seebold. Etymologisches Wörterbuch der deutschen Sprache. 22. Aufl. / Bearb. von Elmar Seebold. ed. Berlin: Walter De Gruyter, 1989.

Tawada has won numerous prizes for her work, such as the Adelbert von Chamisso Prize (1996), the Förderpreis für Literatur der Stadt Hamburg (1990), the Lessingförderpreis (1994), as well as numerous Japanese prizes. She was winner of the prestigious Kleist Prize in 2016.

Tawada writes in a variety of genres and media: novels, poetry, essay collections, plays, and even audio texts. Some of her works are written in Japanese, and then translated into German. Other works are written in German. She rarely translates one language into the other herself, but sometimes writes the same text in both Japanese and German.

Of course Tawada is not alone in making use of multilingualism in her writing. Other multilingual writers writing in German whose works contain the presence of one or more additional languages, include Paul Celan, Franco Biondi, Franz Kafka, Elias Canetti, Galsan Tschinag, Emine Sevgi Özdamar and Tzveta Sofronieva.

Other multilingual works by authors writing in German in the Taylorian Collection:

- Galsan, Chinagiïn. Die graue Erde: Roman. Frankfurt am Main: Insel, 1999.
- Özdamar, Emine Sevgi. Mutterzunge: Erzählungen. Köln: Kiepenheuer & Witsch, 1998.
- Biondi, Franco, and Dragutin. Trumbetas. Im neuen Land. Bremen: CON Medien- und Vertriebsgesellschaft, 1980.
- Celan, Paul, Heino Schmull, and Michael Schwarzkopf. Sprachgitter: Vorstufen, Textgenese, Endfassung. Frankfurt am Main: Suhrkamp Verlag, 1996.

When making deliberate use of several different languages, the way the languages are presented to the reader is a very important consideration. Layout, choice of typeface and clarity of presentation can all influence how the reader perceives the language and culture in relation to others. The Taylorian has examples of bilingual books over several centuries.

Luſthauß	Domicilium recreationis & voluptatis causâ.
Luſtſchif	Navicula luſoria.
Luſtſeuche	Voluptatis libido.

Schottel, Justus Georg. Ausführliche Arbeit Von der Teutschen HaubtSprache/ Worin enthalten Gemelter dieser HaubtSprache Uhrankunft/ Uhraltertuhm/ Reinlichkeit/ Eigenschaft/ Vermögen/ Unvergleichlichkeit/ Grundrichtigkeit/ zumahl die SprachKunst und VersKunst Teutsch und guten theils Lateinisch völlig mit eingebracht/ wie nicht weniger die Verdoppelung/ Ableitung/ die Einleitung/ Nahmwörter/ Authores vom Teutschen Wesen und Teutscher Sprache/ von der verteutschung/ Item die Stammwörter der Teutschen Sprache samt der Erklärung und derogleichen viel merkwürdige Sachen. Abgetheilet In Fünf Bücher. Braunschweig/ Gedrukt und verlegt durch Christoff Friederich Zilligern, 1663.

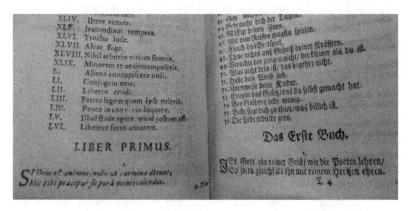

Opitz, Martin, and Esaias Fellgiebel. Des berühmten Schlesiers Martini Opitii von Boberfeld/Bolesl. Opera. Geist- und Weltlicher Gedichte/ nebst beygefügten vielen andern Tractaten so wohl Deutsch als Lateinisch/ Mit Fleiss zusammen gebracht/ und von vielen Druckfehlern befreyet. Die neueste Edition. Breßlau: Verlegts Jesaias Fellgibel, ..., 1690.

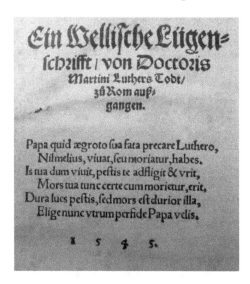

Luther, Martin. *Ein Wellische Lügenschrifft/ von Doctoris Martini Luthers Todt/ zů Rom außgangen. Papa quid ægroto sua fata ... perfide Papa velis. Nürnberg: [Hans Guldenmund], 1545.*

Clifton, E., Friedrich W. Ebeling, and Giovanni. Vitali. *Manuel de la conversation et du style épistolaire : Français-anglais-allemand-italien. Nouv. éd., soigneusement revue et corrigée. ed. Paris: Garnier Frères, 1866.*

English.	French.	Italian.
or else tell them	ou bien dictes leur,	o vero digli,
I will come again	qu' incontinent	che subito
presently	apres soupper	doppo cena
after supper.	je reviendray.	ritornerò.
A. Harkee;	A. Escoutez;	A. Ascolta:
to morrow morning,	demain du matin,	doman la mattina,
before you	devant qu' abbreuviez	prima che dar bere
water my horse,	mon cheval,	al mio cavallo,
carry him to the farrier,	menez le au marefchal,	menalo al marefcalco,
and bid him take care	& dittez lui qu'il fe donne	& di li que guardi bene
not to prick him.	garde de ne l'enclouer.	di non inchiodarlo.
D. Gentlemen,	D. Messieurs,	D. Signori,
do not forget	n'oubliez pas	non dimenticate
to drink to me,	de boire à moy,	di bere a me,
and I will	& je vous	& io vi farò
pledge you all.	faire raifon a tous.	a tutti ragione.
A. Truly you are	A. Certes vous	A. Certo, che havete
to blame	avez tort	gran torto
to break	de rompre	di lafciare
such good company.	fi bonne compagnie.	fi buona compagnia.
D. It cannot		

Taylor, Thomas. The Gentleman's Pocket Companion, for Travelling into Foreign Parts: : Being a Most Easy, Plain and Particular Description of the Roads from London to All the Capital Cities in Europe. With an Account of the Distances of Leagues or Miles from Place to Place, All Reduced to the English Standard. Illustrated with Maps Curiously Engraven on Copper Plates. With Three Dialogues in Six European Languages. The First Being to Ask the Way, with Other Familiar Communications. The Second Is Common Talke in an Inn. The Third Other Necessary Conversation. London: Printed and Sold by Tho: Taylor ..., 1722.

The materiality of the book is a vital aspect of Tawada's works. She experiments with different forms of paper and other materials in her books. Although paper made from plant-based products has been available since the end of the Middle Ages, Tawada chose to have the book cover of *Ein Gedicht für ein Buch* made from fish skin, since fish and water are important in her works.

"When a book is translated into other languages, you can't control the translation." (Yoko Tawada, Jaipur Literary Festival 2016)

Translating Tawada is undoubtedly a challenge; it often requires knowledge of both Japanese and German. It poses many 'problems':

how do we translate neologisms into any language? How do we translate so as to recreate the reading experience of a specific book? For example, in a book that is in German and Japanese, where both languages are to be read in different directions, how is this effect rendered in an English translation? How do we translate into English a German and a Japanese version of the same text?

Tawada's works make us reconsider our own relationship with language, creating the feeling that no-one can be comfortable in any language, even our mother tongue. Is it possible to free oneself from language?

I would like to end this essay with a variety of comments by Yoko Tawada regarding language and translation, taken from Linda Koiran's *Schreiben in Fremder Sprache — Yoko Tawada und Galsan Tschinag* (Munich: Iudicum Verlag, 2009) pp. 257-358 (translations my own):

––––––––

"Wenn man eine weitere Sprache kennt, dann ist die Distanz zwischen sich selbst und der Muttersprache spürbar. Man ist nicht so ganz unter der Macht der Sprache. Das ist eine Befreiung, und dann kann man erst mutig werden."

> If you know another language, then the distance between yourself and the mother tongue can be sensed. You aren't quite so much under the spell of the language. You are released, and only then can you become bold.

"Wenn ich im Denken von der einen Sprache zur anderen springe, spüre ich einen Augenblick stark, dass es ganz dunkle Bereiche gibt, ohne Sprache….Wenn man in diese Kluft einmal hineingefallen ist, dann ist die Muttersprache auch ganz fremd, ich finde Japanish dann sehr komisch und Deutsch sowieso. Dieses Gefühl ist für mich sehr wichtig: sich von der Sprache zu befreien."

> If I jump from one language to another while thinking, I sense for a moment that there are quite dark areas without

language…if you have fallen into this abyss once, then the mother tongue is quite foreign, I then find Japanese very strange, and German too. This feeling for me is very important: to free oneself from language.

"Die literarische Sprache ist sowieso nie die Muttersprache. So wie ich auf Japanisch schreibe, gleicht nicht dem Japanisch, das ich spreche oder der japanischen Sprache, die ich als Kind gelernt habe. In dem Moment, wo man einmal eine Trennung von der Alltagssprache gemacht hat, kommt die literarische Sprache- und die ist sowieso eine Fremdsprache."

Literary language is in any case never the mother tongue. The way I write in Japanese never equates to the Japanese which I speak, or the Japanese language which I learnt as a child. When one has separated from the language of daily use, this is the moment at which literary language arises, and this is in any case a foreign language.

For the following video introductions to the exhibition, please visit: https://www.bodleian.ox.ac.uk/taylor/about/exhibitions-and-publications#tawada

Introduction: On Yoko Tawada
Exhibition Case 2: Bilingual Layout in Yoko Tawada
Exhibition Case 3: Exophonic Writing in German
Exhibition Case 4: Bilingual Layout
Exhibition Case 5: Bilingual Layout 2

Sheela Mahadevan did her BA in French and German at Worcester College, Oxford and her Master's degree at Oriel College, Oxford. She is Deputy Head of Modern Languages at St Olave's Grammar School, Orpington.

Translating Tawada

Alexandra Lloyd

Translation is at the heart of Yoko Tawada's poetics.[1] This makes her a particularly inspiring writer for Oxford students of German, who find themselves week in, week out engaged in the intricate, challenging, and creative process of translating. Tawada's conceptualisation of translation unseats the notion of the original text's superiority, its almost sacred, untouchable quality. In her essay on Paul Celan's poems in Japanese translation, she writes: 'Die Übersetzung ist nicht Abbild des Originals, sondern in ihr bekommt eine Bedeutung des Originals einen neuen Körper' [A translation is not a mirror image of the original, rather through translation the meaning of the original takes on a new form].[2] To take another example: rather than insisting, as many translators and translation theories do, that the new version of a text should bear as little trace of the source language as possible, Tawada sees such traces of the original as an essential part of the translation:

> Für mich besteht der Reiz einer Übersetzung darin, dass sie den Leser die Existenz einer ganz anderen Sprache spüren lässt. Die Sprache der Übersetzung tastet die Oberfläche des Textes vorsichtig ab, ohne sich von seinem Kern abhängig zu machen.[3]

---

[1] On Tawada and translation, see especially Bettina Brandt, 'The Bones of Translation: Yoko Tawada's Translational Poetics', in *Challenging the Myth of Monolingualism*, ed. by Liesbeth Minnaard and Till Dembeck (Leiden and Boston: Brill Rodopi, 2017), pp. 171-80; and Chantal Wright, *Portrait of a Tongue* (Ottawa: University of Ottawa Press, 2013).

[2] Yoko Tawada, 'Das Tor des Übersetzers oder Celan liest Japanisch', in *Talisman* (Tübingen: Konkursbuch, 1996), pp. 121-34 (p. 134); my translation.

[3] Yoko Tawada, 'Schrift einer Schildkröte oder das Problem der Übersetzung', in *Verwandlungen: Tübinger Poetik-Vorlesungen* (Tübingen: Konkursbuch, 1998), pp. 25-40 (pp. 35-36); trans. by Bettina Brandt, 'The Script of a Turtle or the Problem of Translation', in *Challenging the Myth of Monolingualism*, pp. 171-80 (p. 177).

[The appeal of a translation resides for me in providing the reader with a feel for the existence of a totally different language. The language of the translation gently palpates the surface of the text while remaining independent of its nucleus.]

In this same essay, the second of her *Tübinger Poetik-Vorlesungen*, 'Schrift einer Schildkröte oder das Problem der Übersetzung' ['The Script of a Turtle or the Problem of Translation'], Tawada points out that it is easy to criticise a translation, but also easy to praise it for making the reader forget that it is not the 'original' text. This, she suggests, involves a kind of skewed logic: 'Niemand sagt: Diese Literatur ist gut, weil man fast vergisst, dass es Literatur ist' ['Nobody says: this is great literature because you forget that it is literature'].[4] Indeed, Tawada even playfully suggests that perhaps there may be a text from which a supposed 'original' has been translated, or even several of them: '[ich vermute], dass ein literarischer Text später seinen Originaltext finden kann, aus dem er übersetzt worden sein könnte. Meistens existieren mehrere Originaltexte, die gefunden und erfunden werden können' [I suspect that a literary text can later find the original from which it might have been translated. Typically, there are in fact several original texts that can be found or invented].[5]

Tawada's writing was first translated into English by Susan Bernofsky whose recent translation of her novel *Etüden im Schnee* [*Memoirs of a Polar Bear*] has garnered much praise, as well as being awarded the inaugural Warwick Prize for Women in Translation. Bernofsky has commented on Tawada's interest in translation and the effect of that on the translator: 'She will tell you [...]: "Okay, I understand that this language play is not going to work in any other language — go make a language play of your own." She knows that her translators are continuing the writing of the book in the other language,

---

[4] Tawada, 'Schrift einer Schildkröte', p. 35; trans. by Brandt, 'The Script of a Turtle', p. 177.
[5] Ibid, p. 39; ibid, p. 179.

and she enjoys that. She is always about the group project'.[6] It was with this sense of the collaborative and creative nature of translation in mind that on 21 February 2017, students of German and Japanese, and members of the St Edmund Hall Writers' Forum gathered for a translation workshop with Yoko Tawada. The students of German worked on her 2016 essay 'Akzent', while a student from Oriental Studies looked at her Japanese poem 'Why I just can't get up in the morning'.[7] For the students undertaking a creative writing response to Tawada's work, we came up with three prompts drawn from her writings. Thus, the workshop sought to create a truly collaborate space where students could encounter a creative interplay of voices, languages, and ideas.

One of the students, Marcus Li (BA Modern Languages, Magdalen College, 2013-17), was in the process of writing an extended essay on Tawada's poetics, a project that was both academic and personal:

> Reading Tawada's prose brings me back to my childhood of growing up in the 'Zwischenraum' between three languages, when a child's playful gaze is particularly receptive to the oddities behind every-day turns of phrase. That discombobulating sensation, and along with it, the immense creative potential, often has to give way to linguistic conformity in the name of socio-economic integration. 'That isn't how we'd say it in English' or 'what do you mean exactly?' — a scar the outsider must bear. It was exactly this power structure that I wanted to explore through Tawada's German oeuvre. Empowering the linguistically marginalised, her work questions the dichotomy between native and foreign along the axis of

---

[6] Stefanie Sobelle, 'Susan Bernofsky Walks the Tightrope: An Interview About Translating Yoko Tawada's "Memoirs of a Polar Bear"' <https://lareviewof-books.org/article/susan-bernofsky-walks-the-tightrope-an-interview-about-translating-yoko-tawadas-memoirs-of-a-polar-bear/#!> [accessed 29 May 2018].
[7] Both texts appear in full in this volume alongside the students' translations.

creativity, as well as the metaphysical boundaries between the outsider self and their new reality.

Tawada's unique exploration of language considers its limits and possibilities, and the way language shapes identity. Cultural difference is shown to be rich and complex, not straightforward and binary. Yet it is precisely this focus on linguistic and cultural specificity that can make her works a challenge to translate. As Marcus again commented:

> 'Foreignness' is so ingrained in Tawada's aesthetic that the challenge is often not so much about finding a really idiomatic solution to her sentences, but rather how to transport the witty cultural and linguistic contrasts between German and Japanese that she observes into English. When reading, one often has to accept the surreal, almost Kafkaesque assertions her narrators make that hinge on subtle intercultural observations, but when it comes to translating, the underlying logic or word play is tremendously difficult to get across.

The students certainly valued the experience of translating with the author in the room. One undergraduate, Esther Rathbone (BA Modern Languages, St Edmund Hall, 2013-17), was translating Tawada's text 'Gesicht eines Fisches oder das Problem der Verwandlung', the third of her *Tübinger Poetik-Vorlesungen*, for a Special Subject option in Advanced German Translation. Esther commented:

> It's not often that you get the chance to ask an author what they meant with a particular phrase, so this was a valuable opportunity. I found it particularly useful to hear Tawada reading her own work aloud; since her writing is so much about the sound and feel of the German language as spoken by a non-native, it only really made sense when she read it with the intended intonation and pronunciation.

Translating as a group, negotiating different individuals' responses to Tawada's text and approaches to rendering it in English, was also an interesting part of the process. As Esther writes:

It was intriguing to see how other people had interpreted the text and what effects that had on our translations. It definitely brought home to me how beneficial it is to look at literary translation as a fluid and collaborative process. When Tawada didn't have one definitive answer to my questions, it made me realise that there can never be one definitive translation of her work.

Similarly, Marcus commented:

Having Yoko in the room meant that the process of translating literally became a progressive dialogue that pits cultural experiences against one another. Listening to the flow of her voice, the minor breaks and stresses in both English and German helped to make the intended foreignness in the narrative voice more vivid, which helped to bring out the nuances for our translations.

Just as Tawada unsettled the notion of the authority of the source text, so she opened up for students the idea that the author does not have 'solutions' which literary critics and/or translators search for, successfully or in vain. Marcus observed: 'One of the most fulfilling moments during the workshop was when we came up with a translation based on an interpretation of her work that she herself had not even thought of.' For students whose university language work is based heavily on the exercise of translating, this was a radical, exciting, and liberating notion.

At the beginning of the workshop I asked Tawada to tell us about her writing, her processes, and the ways in which translation forms a central part of her poetics. In a mixture of English, German, and Japanese, she shared her thoughts with the group, demonstrating that for her (and, if we chose, for us) the art of translation is so much more than carrying words, perhaps kicking and screaming, from one language system into another. She told us, with what might have been a mischievous smile: 'translation is magic'. As the *Zauberklang* of the students' creative polyphony died away, there was no doubt that she was right.

Akzent. Text and Translation

Yoko Tawada, 'Akzent', translated by Rey Conquer and Chiara Giovanni.

The German text was originally published in *akzentfrei* (Tübingen: Konkursbuch, 2016), pp. 22-29.

Ill. 5/6: Yoko Tawada, Chiara Giovanni (top right) and Rey Conquer (bottom left), translating 'Akzent'

Yoko Tawada

Der Akzent ist das Gesicht der gesprochenen
Sprache. Seine Augen glänzen wie der
Baikalsee oder wie das Schwarze Meer oder
wie ein anderes Wasser, je nachdem, wer
gerade spricht.

Die Augen meiner Sprache enthalten Wasser
aus dem Pazifik, wo zahlreiche Vokale als
Inseln schwimmen. Ohne sie würde ich
ertrinken.

Die deutsche Sprache bietet mir nicht genug
Vokale. „Lufthansa" spreche ich
„Lufutohansa" aus, damit fast jeder
Konsonant mit einem Vokal versorgt ist. Wo
soll ich sonst hin mit meinen Gefühlen, die
nur in den Vokalen zu Hause sind?

Rey Conquer

Accent is the face of spoken language. Its eyes shine like Lake Baikal —, or like the Black Sea, or like some other body of water, depending on who it is that's speaking.

The eyes of my language are filled with water from the Pacific, and vowels, hundreds of them, are islands swimming in it. Without them I would drown.

The German language doesn't have enough vowels for my needs. I have to pronounce 'Lufthansa' *Lufutohansa* so that almost every consonant has its own vowel. Where else am I to put my feelings, when they only feel at home in vowels?

Chiara Giovanni

An accent is the face of the spoken word, eyes sparkling like Lake Baikal or like the Black Sea or like another body of water, depending on who you're listening to as they speak.

The eyes on this face — on my face — hold water from the Pacific, where innumerable vowels swim like islands. Without them, I would drown.

The German language doesn't have nearly enough vowels for me. I pronounce "Lufthansa" like "Lufutohansa" so that nearly every consonant is fitted with its own vowel. What else am I to do with my emotions, which only ever feel at home inside vowels?

Wie würde die Welt aussehen, wenn es nur
Konsonanten gäbe? Sprechen Sie einfach
„k" oder „g" aus, und achten Sie darauf, wie
sie auf Ihren Körper wirken! Sie klingen für
mich nach einer Ablehnung, einer
Abgrenzung oder nach einer leise
gesprochenen Ausrede. Es ist mir
unangenehm, und ich versuche deshalb,
diese Laute mit wenig Druck auszusprechen,
und nehme es in Kauf, dass mein japanischer
Akzent dadurch verstärkt wird. Auch die
expulsiven Konsonanten „p" und „b"
bereiten mir Kopfschmerzen. Sie klingen
verärgert, verachtend und abweisend. Ich
ziehe es vor, beim Aussprechen dieser
Konsonanten die Luft nach innen zu ziehen,
damit sie nicht zu heftig explodieren.

What would the world be like if there were only consonants? Just say *k* or *g* out loud and see what it does to your body. These consonants sound, I think, like a rejection, like a closed border or like a mumbled excuse. I don't like how this feels, and so I try to say them less forcefully and accept that doing so will make my Japanese accent all the stronger. The plosive consonants *p* and *b* give me a headache. They sound cross, scornful and stand-offish. When I pronounce them I would rather draw the air inwards so that they don't make too loud an explosion.

What would the world look like if only consonants existed? All you have to do is say the letter "k" or "g" and see how your body changes. To me, these consonants sound like a rejection, a separation, a whispered justification. I don't like the sensation, and so I attempt to pronounce these sounds with as little force as possible, accepting that my Japanese accent will be stronger, heavier, as a result. Even the plosive consonants "p" and "b" give me a headache. They sound irritable, contemptuous, repulsive. I prefer to inhale when pronouncing these consonants so they don't explode too forcefully.

Es gibt auch sanftere Konsonanten. Das
heißt aber nicht, dass ich sie ohne meinen
Akzent aussprechen könnte. Die
Konsonanten „r" und „l" zum Beispiel
bringe ich durcheinander. Sie sind für mich
eineiige Zwillingsschwestern. Hier einige
Übungen für einen besseren Umgang mit
ihrer Verwechselbarkeit: „Durch das
lustvolle Wandern in der Natur wandelt Herr
Müller seine Gesinnung." „Der Rücken
eines Ponys ist niedrig und deshalb niedlich.
Wäre er doppelt so hoch, wäre er halb so
niedlich." „Kein Bücherregal ist illegal, egal
welche Bücher da stehen, genauso wie kein
Mensch illegal ist, selbst wenn er mit einem
Akzent spricht."

There are also softer consonants. That doesn't mean that I can pronounce them without an accent. For instance, I confuse the consonants *r* and *l*. They're like identical twin sisters. Here are some exercises to help you distinguish between them: 'All roads lead to Rome', 'Mr Miller lights his pipe and writes literary letters.' 'No library is illegal, regardless of which books it holds, just as no human is illegal, even if they speak with an accent.'

There are softer consonants, too. That does not mean, however, that I can pronounce them without my accent coming through. I always, for example, mix up the consonants "r" and "l". They are identical twin sisters to me. Below are some exercises to familiarise yourself with their interchangeability: *Yellow arrows frilled with reefed leaves are rarely light. It's the right light with the glimmer in the mirror. An accent can be loyal or even sound royal, no matter how many corrections need to be collected. Speaking with an accent is not a crime.*

Der Akzent bringt unerwartet zwei Wörter zusammen, die normalerweise nicht ähnlich klingen. In meinem Akzent hören sich die „Zelle" und die „Seele" ähnlich an.

Es ist nicht meine Aufgabe, eine regionale Färbung, einen ausländischen Akzent, einen Soziolekt und einen Sprachfehler medizinischer Art voneinander zu unterscheiden. Stattdessen schlage ich vor, jede Abweichung als eine Chance für die Poesie wahrzunehmen.

Accents bring words unexpectedly together which wouldn't usually sound the same. In my accent 'cell' and 'sail' sound almost identical.

I'm not here to distinguish between a regional colouring, a foreign accent, a sociolect and a speech disorder. Instead I want to suggest that every deviation should be seen as a chance for poetry.

My accent unexpectedly brings two words together that don't normally sound alike; with my accent, "cell" and "soul" sound alike.

I do not seek to differentiate between regional colour, foreign accents, sociolects, and medical speech defects. Instead, I propose that we see every instance of deviance as an opportunity for poetry.

Es kommt mir komisch vor, dass ich von einer „Abweichung" spreche, denn ich bin nicht sicher, ob es überhaupt den „Standard" gibt. Im Sprachunterricht in Japan habe ich gelernt, dass das reinste Hochdeutsch in Hannover zu finden sei, und zwar auf einer Theaterbühne und nicht irgendwo auf der Straße. Aber es gibt keinen Menschen, der in einem Hannoveraner Theater geboren wurde und nie das Theatergebäude verlassen hat. Also gibt es keinen Menschen ohne Akzent, so wie es keinen Menschen ohne Falten im Gesicht gibt. Der Akzent ist das Gesicht der gesprochenen Sprache, und ihre Falten um die Augen und in der Stirn zeichnen jede Sekunde eine neue Landschaft. Der Sprecher hat all diese fernen Landschaften durchlebt, mitgeprägt, vertont, mitgestaltet, ernährt, unterstützt, vielleicht auch zerstört, und das zeigt sich in seiner Aussprache. Sein Akzent ist seine Autobiographie, die rückwirkend in die neue Sprache hineingeschrieben wird.

It feels odd to talk of a 'deviation' as I'm not sure that there is anything like a 'standard'. In language classes in Japan I learnt that the purest German is to be found in Hannover, and particularly on the stage, rather than on the street. But no one has ever been born in a theatre in Hannover and then never left the building. This means that there is no one without an accent, in the same way that there is no one without wrinkles on their face. Accent is the face of spoken language and the wrinkles around its eyes and on its forehead draw, from one second to the next, the contours of a new landscape. The speaker has lived through all these distant landscapes, has left their mark on them, set them to music, has helped shape them, helped feed them, supported them, perhaps also destroyed them, and that shows in their pronunciation. Their accent is an autobiography, written retrospectively into the new language.

It seems odd to speak of *deviance*, given that I'm unsure of whether such thing as a *norm* even exists. In German lessons in Japan I learned that the purest form of German can be heard in Hannover, and not just anywhere on the street, but in the theatre — on stage, to be precise. But there is not a person alive who was born in a Hannover theatre and never left. So there is not a person alive without an accent, just as there is not a person alive without wrinkles on their face. An accent is the face of the spoken word, and the crow's-feet around its eyes and the frown lines on its forehead paint a new landscape with every second that passes. The speaker has lived through all these far-flung landscapes, has changed them, lent them sound, shape, has nourished them, supported them, perhaps even destroyed them, and all that is there in their accent. An accent is an autobiography, retrospectively written in the new language.

Der Akzent ist eine großzügige Einladung zu einer Reise in die geografische und kulturelle Ferne. In einer modernen Großstadt muss man stets darauf gefasst sein, mitten in der Mittagspause auf eine Weltreise geschickt zu werden. Eine Kellnerin öffnet ihren Mund, schon bin ich unterwegs nach Moskau, nach Paris oder nach Istanbul. Die Mundhöhle der Kellnerin ist der Nachthimmel, darunter liegt ihre Zunge, die den eurasischen Kontinent verkörpert. Ihr Atemzug ist der Orientexpress. Ich steige ein.

An accent is a generous invitation to journey to a geographically and culturally distant place. In a modern city you must always be ready — during your lunch break, for instance — to be sent off on a trip around the world. A barista opens her mouth and I'm already on my way to Moscow, to Paris or Istanbul. The barista's mouth is the night sky, and under it is her tongue, the Eurasian continent. Her breath is the Orient Express. I climb aboard.

An accent is a bold, open-hearted invitation on a geographical and cultural voyage to faraway places. Nowadays, if you live in a major city, you have to be prepared to be transported halfway across the world in the middle of your lunch break. The waitress opens her mouth to speak, and there — I'm already en route to Moscow, Paris, Istanbul. The waitress' mouth is the night sky, below it lies her tongue, encompassing the Eurasian contient. Her intake of breath is the Orient Express, and it's boarding.

Wer mit Akzent spricht, fühlt sich zu Hause. Der Akzent ist seine Eigentumswohnung im wahren Sinne des Wortes, denn er ist sein Eigentum, das ihm selbst in der Zeit der Wirtschaftskrise nicht abhandenkommt. Er trägt ihn immer mit sich im Mund und kann somit immer in den eigenen vier Wänden gemütlich seine Fremdsprache sprechen.

Gäbe es keinen Akzent mehr, bestünde die Gefahr, dass man schnell vergisst, wie unterschiedlich die Menschen sind.

Anyone who speaks with an accent feels at home. An accent is like a house you have bought, your possession in the true sense of the word, something that, even in times of economic crisis, cannot be lost. It's something you always have with you — in your mouth — and so you can always speak a foreign language in the comfort of your own four walls.

If there stopped being accents we would run the risk of forgetting all too soon how different people are.

If you speak with an accent, you will always feel at home. Your accent is your asset in the truest sense of the word, because it's your property, and not even a recession can repossess it, can take it away from you. You carry it with you inside your mouth and will thus always be able to speak your foreign language within the comfort of your own four walls. If there were no more accents, there would be the danger of too easily forgetting how diverse people can be.

Der Akzent gibt den Menschen auch Mut, denn er ist ein lebender Beweis dafür, dass auch ein Erwachsener noch eine ganz exotische Sprache lernen kann. Hätte er sie schon als kleines Kind gelernt, hätte er keinen Akzent. Auch im hohen Alter können wir unseren Gaumen erweitern, uns neue fiktive Zähne wachsen lassen, die Muskeln des Mundwerkes trainieren, mehr Speichel produzieren und unsere Gehirnzellen durchkneten und durchlüften. Das Ziel der Sprachlernenden ist nicht, sich dem Zielort anzupassen. Man kann immer wieder eine neue Sprache lernen und die alten Sprachen als Akzent beibehalten.

An accent can be a source of encouragement: as it is living proof that even as an adult you can learn a language quite new to you. If you had learnt it as a child then you wouldn't have an accent. But even when old we can widen our gums, allow new, imaginary teeth to grow, train the muscles of our mouths, produce more saliva and give our brain cells a kneading and an airing. People don't learn a language with the aim of becoming completely assimilated into it. You can learn language after language and keep the old ones as an accent.

An accent also gives you courage, because it's living proof that even adults can still learn a brand new language. If you'd learnt the language as a child, you wouldn't have an accent. So even in our ripe old age, we can enlarge our mouths, extend our gums, cut new teeth, so to speak, train up the muscles in our mouth, produce more saliva, air out and knead up our brain cells. Language learners are not aiming for total assimilation into the target location. You can always learn a new language and keep the old ones as an accent.

Wer keinen Akzent hat und nicht fremd
aussieht, aber aus der Ferne kommt, hat es
schwer. Die Tochter meiner deutschen
Bekannten zum Beispiel, die in den USA
geboren und aufgewachsen ist, hatte Angst,
in Deutschland zum Postamt zu gehen. Denn
sie hat gar keinen Akzent, wenn sie Deutsch
spricht, aber sie versteht nur noch Bahnhof,
wenn   der   Postangestellte   von
„Einschreiben", „Nachnahme" oder „unfrei"
spricht. Hätte sie einen Akzent, würde man
ihr verständnisvoll in Ruhe diese Wörter
erklären. Aber sie hat leider gar keinen
Akzent. Sie sagte mir, man würde denken,
sie sei nicht ganz „dicht".

People who don't have an accent and don't look foreign but come from other parts of the world have a hard time. The daughter of a German acquaintance, for example, who was born and grew up in the USA, is afraid of going to the post office in Germany. She has no accent at all when she speaks German, but it's all Greek to her when the assistant says things like 'registered letter' 'payment on delivery' or 'freight forward'. If she had an accent people would explain these terms to her slowly and sympathetically. But — unfortunately — she doesn't have an accent. She tells me that people think that she's not all there.

People who don't have an accent and don't look foreign, but who come from faraway, have it tough. A German friend's daughter, for example, who was born and raised in the US, is too scared to go to the post office in Germany. She has no accent when speaking German, but she's completely lost when the person at the counter starts talking about "signatures", "surnames" or "recorded delivery". If she had an accent, the member of staff would patiently explain all these words to her. But, unfortunately for her, she has no accent. She tells me that people would think she wasn't quite "right" in the head.

Es kann für mehrsprachige Dichterinnen und Dichter ein Vorteil sein, wenn die Wände in ihrem Gehirn „nicht ganz dicht" sind. Durch die undichte Wand sickert der Klang einer Sprache in eine andere hinein und erzeugt eine atonale Musik. [...]

Es gibt Menschen, die einen Sprecher mit Akzent unbewusst abwerten. Kaum hören sie einen fremden Sprachklang, schon werden in ihnen Hormone ausgeschüttet, die als Gefahrensignal ihre Gehirnzellen erreichen. Ich weiß nicht, ob diese Gene aus der Steinzeit stammen oder durch die modernen Massenmedien manipuliert sind. Dabei ist die Geschichte voll von positiven Erfahrungen mit fremdländischen Akzenten. Ohne Menschen mit niederländischem Akzent wäre zum Beispiel die deutsche Hauptstadt heute noch ein Sumpf. [...]

For multilingual poets it can be an advantage if the walls in their heads are not all there. Through the gaps, the sound of one language seeps into another and generates a kind of atonal music.

There are people who unconsciously look down on those who speak with an accent. They've hardly heard a foreign-sounding voice and the hormones have already poured out and are sounding the alarm in their brain cells. I don't know if these genes go all the way back to the Stone Age or have somehow been manipulated by modern mass media. At the same time, history is full of positive experiences with foreign accents. Without people with a Dutch accent, for example, the capital of Germany would still be a swamp.

It can be an advantage for multilingual writers if they aren't *quite right*. The lack of *rightness*, of *uprightness*, allows the diagonal sound of another language to make its way through and weave together a piece of atonal music.

There are people who unconsciously judge people with accents. No sooner does the foreign intonation reach their ears than are hormones released that reach their brain cells as danger signals. I'm not sure whether these genes are a relic of the Stone Age, or whether they're manipulated by the modern media. In any case, history is full of positive testimonies to foreign accents. Without people with a Dutch accent, for instance, the German capital would still be a swamp.

Man spricht heutzutage vom „Migrations-
hintergrund", als wäre etwas Abgründiges
grundsätzlich hinter dem Rücken versteckt.
Der Akzent ist der *Vordergrund* der
Migration. [...]

Zum Glück schaffen wir es nie, ganz ohne
jeden Akzent zu sprechen. Sonst würde
unsere Sprache farblos, angepasst,
uninteressant, verklemmt, steif, ängstlich,
monoton oder kalt klingen. Sie wäre dann
nur noch ein verfaulter Überrest von dem,
was die gesprochene Sprache sein kann.

Nowadays people in Germany use the phrase 'migration *back-ground*' as if there were something mysterious hiding behind a migrant's back. Accent is rather the *foreground* of migration.

Luckily, we will never manage to speak without an accent. Without accents our language would sound colourless, conforming, uninteresting, uptight, stiff, nervous, monotonous or cold. It would then be nothing but a decaying relic of what a spoken language can be.

Nowadays we speak of people being "of foreign origin", as though one's heritage were something to be left behind, at the start, instead of being carried with you. An accent is not part of the origin, but of the journey.

Fortunately, we will never lose our accents entirely. If we did, our speech would sound colourless, assimilated, uninteresting, cramped, stiff, anxious, monotonous, cold. All that would remain would be the rotten excess of what the spoken word has the potential to be.

About the translators

Rey Conquer is a Laming Junior Fellow at The Queen's College, Oxford. Their doctoral thesis looked at colour in poetry in the early twentieth century, and they are currently working on a project about ideas of space in modernist church design and concrete poetry. They have published on translation technique in Stefan George's *Shakespeare. Sonnette* and have translated, with Izabela Rakar, parts of Thomas Kling's cycle 'Der erste Weltkrieg', for which they were commended in the 2016 Stephen Spender Prize.

Chiara Giovanni is a PhD student of Comparative Literature at Stanford University, and holds undergraduate and masters degrees in Modern Languages from the University of Oxford. Chiara is interested in sites of encounter between English- and Spanish-speaking worlds, and the cultural production of the Spanish Caribbean and its diaspora. She works with theories of emotion, desire, and affect, and is currently thinking about love as a method of identity formation, particularly for marginal subjects.

Ill. 7: The translation workshop at St Edmund Hall, 21 February 2017

Japanese Texts

1. 'Fukushima', first published in the Hokkaidō newspaper, 6 March 2016, p. 11. Original title: 「書くことと旅すること　福島の喪失感、小説で形に」('Kaku koto to tabi suru koto. Fukushima no sōshitsukan, shōsetsu de katachi ni').

2. 'Saitama', unpublished.

3. 'Why I just can't get up in the morning', first published in Gendaishi techō 59.1 (2016), p. 150f. Original title: 「朝なかなか起きられない理由」('Asa nakanaka okirarenai riyū').

About the translator

Lucy Fleming-Brown studied Japanese as part of a BA in Oriental Studies at the University of Oxford. During that time, she spent one year abroad at Kobe University (Japan), where she majored in Art History. She is particularly interested in Japanese post-war photography and creative dissent.

1. Fukushima

　　ひろ子さんの家は、背の高い雑草に覆われていた。中に入った途端、湿った悲しい空気を肌に感じた。その家はまるで感情を持つ生き物みたいだった。台所の床には棚から落ちて砕けた食器の破片が散らばっていた。テーブルの上に四角いお皿が一枚置いてあって、上に不思議な物体が乗っていた。

　　「これ、何だかわかりますか。」

　　ひろ子さんにそう訊かれ、顔を近づけてよく見たが、何なのか見当もつかなかった。

　　「あの日の朝、娘に焼いてあげた卵焼きなんです。わざとそのままにしておいてあるんです。」

　　あの日というのは２０１１年３月１１日のことである。すっかり水分が蒸発し、卵焼きは化石のようになっている。四年以上も前につくられた卵焼きを見るのは初めてだった。

　　「家が流されてしまった人を羨ましく思うことさえあります。もう決してこの家に戻ることはないと分かっていても、取り壊すことはできないし、少しずつ壊れていくのをただ見ているしかない。それがつらくて。来るのはもうやめようと何度も思ったんですけれど、やっぱり来てしまうんです。」

　　ここは福島県浪江町。過去をきれいに葬って、新しく出直す方がいいと思う人もいるだろう。でもひろ子さんにとっては忘れてしまうわけにはいかない何かがあり、記憶を形にして残しておきたいという気持ちが強くあったから、卵焼きを残して置いたのだろう。原爆ドームのように大きな記念碑でなくても、人は何か歴史を振り返る手がかりになる物を必要とする。

1. Fukushima

Hiroko's house was hidden by tall weeds. Just as you came in, you felt the damp, sad air under your skin. It was as if the house was a living thing, with its own feelings. On the kitchen floor, fragments of tableware, which had fallen from a shelf and smashed, were scattered. On the table, a square plate had been placed, upon which a mysterious object was raised.

"Do you know what this is?"

Hiroko asked, and although I drew my face close and looked hard, I had no idea what it was.

"This is an omelette, that I cooked and gave my daughter the morning of that day. I have left it there like that on purpose."

As for that day, that was the 11th of March, 2011. The water content had completely evaporated, and the omelette had become a fossil.

It was the first time that I had seen an omelette which had been made four years before.

"I even envy the people whose houses were washed away. Even though I knew that I would never return to this house again, I am unable to pull it down, so I have no choice but to just watch as it is ruined little by little. That's painful. Despite having thought many times that by now I should stop coming, I still come anyway."

This is Namiemachi in Fukushima prefecture. There might be people who think we should bury the past cleanly, and make a fresh start. However, for Hiroko, there are some things which we cannot afford to forget completely, and I think that it might be because she feels strongly that she would like the memory to remain in tact as a form, that the omelette stays placed there. Even if it is not a great memorial like the Atom Bomb Dome, it's essential for people that there is something which acts as a means by which to look back on history.

ひろ子さんと近所を少し散歩した。「ゴーストタウン」という言葉が浮かんだ。住んでいる人は誰もいないが、特別許可証をもらえば数時間入ることができる。近くに新聞の配達所があり、２０１１年３月１１日の新聞が積みあげられていた。あの日に配達されるはずだった新聞だ。

I wandered the neighbourhood with Hiroko for a little while. The word 'Ghost town' came to mind. There was nobody living there, but if you received a special permit, you could come in for a couple of hours. Nearby, there was a newspaper delivery place, and the newspapers for the 11th of March, 2011, had been piled up. They were the newspapers that had been intended for delivery that day.

2. Saitama

（切断されたコード）
発汗する渋谷と
火傷する福島の間を
強引に結ぶ一直線を
わたしたちは埼玉で切断する
こともできる。
電流を断ち切って
脳味噌を発電所に変える
ことも。

（スピーカー）
あなたの声を
大きくするための
媒介
であるはずなのに
自分の宣伝ばかり
している。

（音量調整）
ボリュームを上げていこう。
死者の声が聞こえるまで。

（壁のひび）
向こう側があるから
ヒビができる。
いつか壁が崩れて
あれが出てくる。

2. Saitama

(The cut off cord)
Between sweating Shibuya and
scalding Fukushima
the violently binding straight line is one
that we, at Saitama, can cut.
We can also cut the electrical supply
turn brains into power stations.

(Speaker)
Even though it was meant to be
a transmitter
for the sake of making your voice louder
it only
promotes itself.

(Volume Adjustment)
Let us raise the volume
Until the voices of the dead can be heard.

(The wall's crack)
Because there is another side
It can crack.
At some point walls crumble
It's coming out.

（黴）
身を寄せ合い
オシクラ饅頭都市で
はじき合って生きる
フンマリした白あん。
ネットりした黒あん。
栄養過多の寂しさで
顔を膨らまし
共生している。

(Mold)
Bodies coming together
In the marble game town
Living, bumping off each other
Spongey white bean paste
Gummy black bean paste
Through overeating's loneliness
With swelled faces
United.

3. 朝なかなか起きられない理由

沼の表面を割って咲く
蓮の花のように
ぱりっと目をあけると
顔が踏みつぶされてグジャグジャだ
無数の靴がわたしの上を歩いていった
幾世代も続いた夜があっけなく終わり
照明係にスポットライトをあてられて
なんだ夢だったんだと
すっきり何もかも忘れていいはずなのに
沼になってしまった顔が元にもどらない
自分探しはやめて犯人を捜そう
君がわるいんじゃない、どんな沼顔でも恥ずかしくはない
さ
犯人たちの靴のサイズは平均二センチ半
革靴は値段が高いほど踏まれる側は痛い
スパイクのついた靴を履いていたのは主婦のサッカー・チ
ームの人たち
一番痛いのはファッショ！モデルのハイヒールの踵
昼間はやさしくしてくれる人たちがなぜ
寝ている間にわたしの顔を踏みしだいていくのか
それとも長すぎた釘が金槌で打たれ続けるうちに棺桶の蓋
を突き抜けて
わたしの顔に次々刺さっていったのか
夜が更けると、もう寝なさいという声が聞こえる
経帷子に着替えたくない
歯ブラシで前歯に死に化粧をほどこしたくない
時限爆弾みたいな目覚まし時計を仕掛けたくない
就寝前に行われるあらゆる儀式がいとわしい
立ったまま眠りたい

3. Why I just can't get up in the morning

Splitting the surface of the mire blooming
Like a lotus flower
I crack my eyes open
And my face is trampled, torn up
Countless shoes stepped over me
Even a night lasting generations ends too soon
Hit by the spotlight thrown out by the illuminator
It was just a dream
Even though I thought I could completely forget it all
My face, which became a mire, does not change back to what it was
Stop the self-search, go and hunt the culprit
It's not that you're bad, however mired your face, no need to be embarrassed
The size of the culprits' shoes are an average two and a half centimeters
The higher the price of the leather shoes, the more the trampled side hurts
In spiked shoes, a housewives' football team
The greatest pain is Fasho Models' high heels
In the daytime they are gentle to me
Why whilst I sleep, do they step on my face
Or did they strike with too long nails, driving through the casket's cover
One after another piercing my face
As the night draws on You must sleep says a voice I can hear
I have no wish to take up the white kimono of the dead
I do not want to make up my front teeth for death with my toothbrush
I do not want to start the time bomb like alarm clock
Before going to bed, each ceremony required is hateful
Standing, I want to sleep

たとえば二十四時間営業の地下鉄の中で
帰る家のない人たちの間でもまれて
暖かい身体に四方から押されて
よろめくことなく垂直に眠りたい

As if amongst the 24 hour service of the underground
Pushed around by the people with no home to turn back to
Warm bodies from each direction pushing me up
Without swaying, vertically I want to sleep